HARDKNOTT CASTLE
AND THE
TENTH ANTONINE ITINERARY

—

BY

R. G. COLLINGWOOD ESQ.,

M.A., F.S.A.

British Library Cataloguing-in-Publication Data
A catalogue record for this book is available from
the British Library

R. G. Collingwood

Robin George Collingwood was born on 22nd February 1889, in Cartmel, England. He was the son of author, artist, and academic, W. G. Collingwood.

Collingwood attended Rugby School before enrolling at University College, Oxford, where he received a congratulatory first class honours for reading Greats. He became a fellow of Pembroke College, Oxford, and remained there for 15 years until he was offered the post of Waynflete Professor of Metaphysical Philosophy at Magdalen College, Oxford. He was greatly influenced by the Italian Idealists Croce, Gentile, and Guido de Ruggiero. Another important influence was his father, a professor of fine art and a student of Ruskin.

Collingwood produced *The Principles of Art* in 1938, outlining the concept of art as being essentially expressions of emotion. He claimed that it was a necessary function of the human mind and considered it an important collaborative activity. He also published other works of philosophy, such as *Speculum Mentis* (1924), *An Essay on Philosophic Method* (1933), *An Essay on Metaphysics* (1940), and many more. In 1940, he published *The First Mate's Log,* an account of a sailing trip he undertook with some of his students in the Mediterranean.

Collingwood died at Coniston, Lancashire on January 1943, after a series of debilitating strokes.

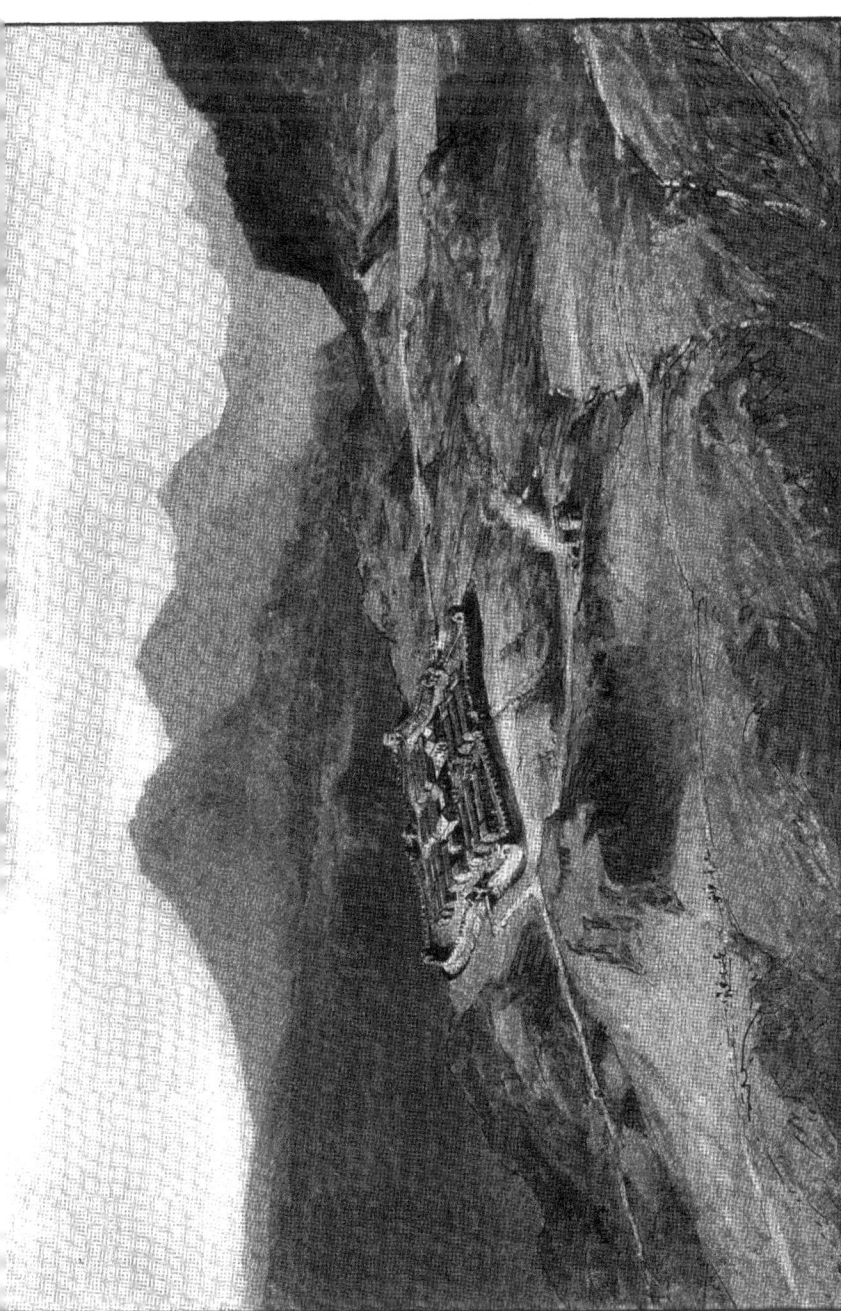

W. G. Collingwood

HARDKNOT CASTLE AND THE SCAFELL RANGE

Published by the Society of Antiquaries of London, 1922

I.—*Hardknot Castle and the Tenth Antonine Itinerary.*
By R. G. COLLINGWOOD, *Esq., M.A., F.S.A.*

Read 27th January 1921.

THE Tenth Iter[1] in the British section of the Antonine road-book has been for many years—indeed for centuries—a standing puzzle in Romano-British history. Of its nine stations the seventh, Mancunium, has always been recognized as Manchester; but the others are not so easily identifiable. The first, third, and fifth reappear in the *Notitia Dignitatum* towards the end of the section headed *item per lineam valli*; but it has long been admitted by every one that they are not therefore necessarily to be sought on Hadrian's Wall itself. Camden, on the strength of an inscription found by Reginald Bainbrigg at Whitley Castle near Alston, identified that fort with Alone, the third station of the Iter; and Horsley, accepting this identification, made the Iter begin at Lanchester and traverse a series of stations lying behind Hadrian's Wall and acting as supports to it, before turning south by way of the Eden and Lune valleys to Manchester. That was a good solution, and indeed the best possible solution, granted the correctness of the equation Alone = Whitley Castle; but it necessitated the complete rejection of the mileages as given in the Iter, since the hundred statute miles from Whitley to Manchester are represented by 83 Roman miles or about 76 statute miles between Alone and Mancunium. Moreover, Camden's identification was unsound. The *Notitia* places the Third Cohort of Nervii at Alone (spelt in that document Alione) and Bainbrigg's inscription mentioned the Second Cohort. Camden arbitrarily altered the numeral in order to effect the identification.[2]

Horsley's reading of the Iter thus falls to the ground; indeed, his treatment of the mileages was so high-handed that even before Camden's falsification of the Whitley inscription had been detected (in 1911) there had arisen a general feeling of dissatisfaction with Horsley's solution of the problem. The result was

[1] For the reader's convenience I repeat the names and Roman mileages. Clanoventa-18-Galava-12-Alone-19-Calacum-27-Bremetonacum-20-Coccium-17-Mancunium-18-Condate-19-Mediolanum.
[2] *Cumb. and West. Trans.* N.S. xi, p. 359; *Eph. Epigr.* ix, p. 566. The inscription is *C.I.L.* vii, 310.

a crop of fresh solutions, differing from Horsley chiefly for the worse. Horsley himself having set the example of maltreating the Itinerary mileages, others felt themselves at liberty to do the same without the same motive; and the imaginative re-identification of the Tenth Iter became a recognized form of sport among local antiquaries.

The results achieved up to thirty years ago were tabulated by Chancellor Ferguson in his *History of Cumberland* (pp. 51–2). The sight of a dozen incompatible solutions, printed side by side without comment, may have been intended as an ironical warning to any one who might be tempted to increase their number; and this is the effect which it seems to have produced, for English antiquaries began to see that the sport in question had its dangers, and to resist its attractions. For this reason it is unnecessary to rescue from their oblivion the solutions which Chancellor Ferguson pilloried; but it may be desirable to mention one of these purely imaginative solutions, because it has appeared within the last few years in a work which on the face of it seems to carry a good deal of authority and is likely to mislead.

Professor Konrad Miller's *Itineraria Romana* is a folio of 1,000 pages dealing with the entire road-system of the Roman Empire, and published at Stuttgart in 1916. The Tenth Iter is in this work identified as follows. From Manchester (the eighth and ninth stations do not concern us here) it is made to proceed to Coccium at Ribchester (28 Roman miles as against the Itinerary distance of 18), and thence to Bremetonacum at Lancaster (24 Roman miles, Itinerary 20 miles). The *Notitia Dignitatum* places at Bremetonacum a *cuneus armaturarum*, and this is often taken to be a corruption of *cuneus Sarmatarum*, because from *C. I. L.* vii, 218 and 230, we know Ribchester to have been garrisoned by Sarmatian cavalry. But Professor Miller, ignoring both this and the further fact that Lancaster was garrisoned by the Gaulish Ala Sebosiana or Sebussiana (*C. I. L.* vii, 287; tile, *C. I. L.* vii, p. 70) ascribes the Sarmatian garrison to Lancaster on no evidence whatever (since if Bremetonacum is not Ribchester there is no reason for emending *armaturarum* to *Sarmatarum*) and clean against the very good lapidary evidence both at Ribchester and at Lancaster.

The next stage of Professor Miller's itinerary is to Calacum, which he places at 'Hawkshead am Windermere-See, mit römischen Altertümern', from which, he says, come certain inscriptions (*C. I. L.* vii, 291, 292). Now there is a fort on the shore of Windermere, at Ambleside, otherwise known as Waterhead; this is about 32 miles (Roman) from Lancaster as against 27 in the Iter. There is also a village called Hawkshead, five miles away and well off the lake, with no Roman remains or even roads near it; but a Roman coin was once found there, and is recorded by Mr. H. Swainson Cowper, F.S.A., in his 'Archaeological Survey of Lancashire north of the Sands', published by this Society (*Archaeologia*,

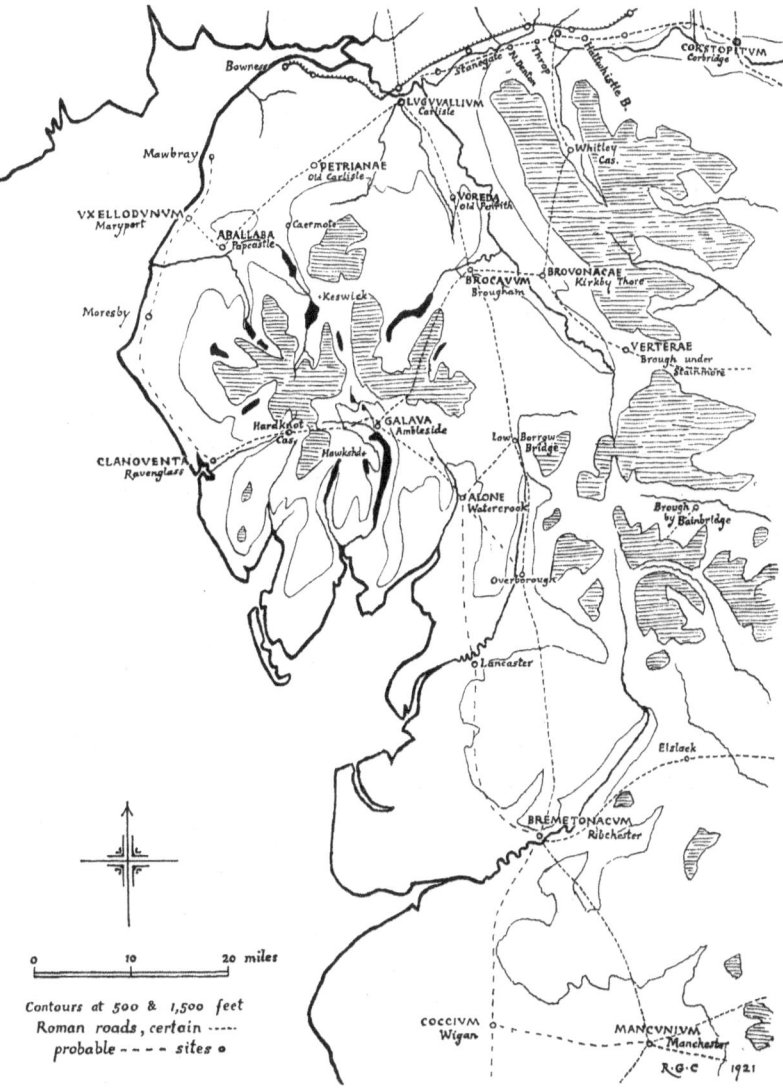

Fig. 1. Map to illustrate the Tenth Iter.

liii, p. 535). Further, there is a Roman fort (described in *Cumb. and West. Trans.* N.S. viii, pp. 102–8) at Watercrook near Kendal, twelve miles away in another direction, to which Hübner explicitly and correctly ascribed the two inscriptions placed by Miller at Hawkshead. It thus appears that, confused by the similarity of name, Professor Miller has identified Watercrook, Waterhead, and Hawkshead, has called them collectively by the name of the least important, and has moved this site five miles to the shores of Windermere. After this, it is surprising to observe that they are all three entered separately and correctly on his own map.

So far Professor Miller has confined himself to real forts and real or at least highly probable roads. He now abandons the last restraints of fact and takes his next stage (15 Roman miles, Itinerary 19 miles) over Dunmail Raise to Keswick. Between the shore of Windermere and Keswick there is no Roman road, and no responsible person has ever claimed to have identified one; but there is certainly an old traffic-line which Chancellor Ferguson rather rashly marked in his Archaeological Survey of Cumberland and Westmorland,[1] together with a great number of others, as a line that might possibly have been Roman. At Keswick there is no vestige of a Roman site of any kind, though a scrap or two of Romano-British pottery and glass has been found. Another wholly imaginary road (13 miles, Itinerary 12) takes Professor Miller to Papcastle, a real Roman fort called Aballaba (*Notitia*), Aballava (*C. I. L.* vii, 415), or Avalana (Ravennas), which he is compelled to identify with Galava. On the strength of the Ravennas spelling it would perhaps have been easier to identify it with Alone, especially as the Ravennas has a variant Alauna which Miller in point of fact accepts; but that name has been bestowed on the non-existent fort at Keswick, and there is nothing for it but to assume that Galava and Aballaba are variant spellings of one and the same name. Hence a final stage (25 miles, Itinerary 18 miles) leads to Bowness-on-Solway, the terminal station of Hadrian's Wall, which must therefore be Clanoventa. Part of the road is imaginary, but evidence for it is found in a mistake of Hübner, who

---

[1] The groundwork of Professor Miller's theory seems to be derived from this Survey, ignoring all later work on the subject. In its first form in 1883 (*Cumb. and West. Trans.* O.S. iii, pp. 69 *sqq.*) that work took the Tenth Iter by Ambleside and Keswick to end at Old Carlisle; at that date it was still possible to put forward such a view in spite of the admitted absence of remains of any kind between Ambleside and Papcastle, and even then critics were not wanting who pointed out the entire baselessness of the identification. In its later form in 1889 (*Archaeologia*, vol. liii) it entered the road by Keswick as merely 'probable', and the identification of this road with the Tenth Iter was tacitly withdrawn. Most of the 'probable' roads in the 1889 map are either baseless conjecture or based on misinterpreted evidence; indeed, the reference given for the Roman road to Keswick (s.v. Grasmere) is to an article by C. Nicholson pointing out quite correctly that reasons for believing in such a road were wholly wanting. The plea that Professor Miller relied for his facts on Chancellor Ferguson is therefore inadmissible.

transferred to this part of Cumberland the milestone found at Hangingshaw near Appleby (*C. I. L.* vii, 1179; *Cumb. and West. Trans.* N.S. xvi, p. 132).

The year before this latest and most irresponsible of the imaginative solutions was published, a paper had appeared entitled 'The Romano-British Names of Ravenglass and Borrans (Muncaster and Ambleside)' in the *Archaeological Journal* (1915, vol. lxxii), in which the late Professor Haverfield argued that Clanoventa, Galava, and Alone were Ravenglass, Ambleside, and Watercrook near Kendal. The distances (18 miles from Ravenglass to Ambleside, 12 thence to Watercrook) are precisely those of the Itinerary. From Kendal to Ribchester, whether by Lancaster or by Overborough, is about 40 miles, which is too short to correspond with the 46 miles from Alone to Bremetonacum, and Haverfield suggested that Calacum, the fourth station, was Lancaster and that the roads, which are hereabouts not accurately known, were rather circuitous. He selected Lancaster because the road by way of that fort would be a mile or two longer than that by Overborough. But even so the distances do not really come right, and if the theory is to be satisfactorily worked out it seems necessary either to emend the XIX between Alone and Calacum to XI, placing Calacum at Overborough, or to emend the XXVII between Calacum and Bremetonacum to XXII, in which case Calacum will be Lancaster. Either emendation would satisfy the requirements and bring the distances of the Iter to within a quite reasonable margin of error.

Setting aside the problem of the fourth station, however, the identification of the first three was convincing. Ravenglass, with its magnificent harbour, a land-locked lagoon formed by the confluence of three rivers in a single estuary, makes a good terminus for a route; and the evidence from the *Notitia Dignitatum* and the Ravenna Cosmography goes to confirm its identification with Clanoventa. The reason why no one had previously hit on this solution of the problem was very simple. Midway between Ravenglass and Ambleside is the fort locally known as Hardknot Castle, perched 800 feet above the sea on a spur of Hardknot mountain, a precipice flanking it on one side and an impassable ravine on the other, commanding the whole of Eskdale and blocking the pass by which the road runs inland to Ambleside. It lies in the middle of the finest mountain scenery in England, protected by its position from stone-robbing and from the plough, and in a place much visited by many kinds of tourists; moreover, it was brought into public notice by being dug in the years 1889–93 (*Cumb. and West. Trans.* O.S. xii). Thus Hardknot is an exceptionally well-known site, and any one who felt inclined to identify the Ambleside-Ravenglass road with the Tenth Iter would naturally make it his first object to find a name for Hardknot. But this the mileages of the Itinerary do not permit.

The originality of Haverfield's identification lay in the fact that he ignored

Hardknot. The paper in which he expounded his view did not even mention its name. Now this was the obvious weak point of the theory. Every reader of the paper would at once raise the question, what about Hardknot, and why is it omitted from the Itinerary? It is true that other Itineraries pass over sites. Iters II and V traverse the same road between Carlisle and Brough-under-Stainmore, but of the three intervening forts Iter II omits Brougham, while Iter V omits the other two, Kirkby Thore and Old Penrith. There are, of course, other cases, such as the omission of Lanchester in Iter I. But the

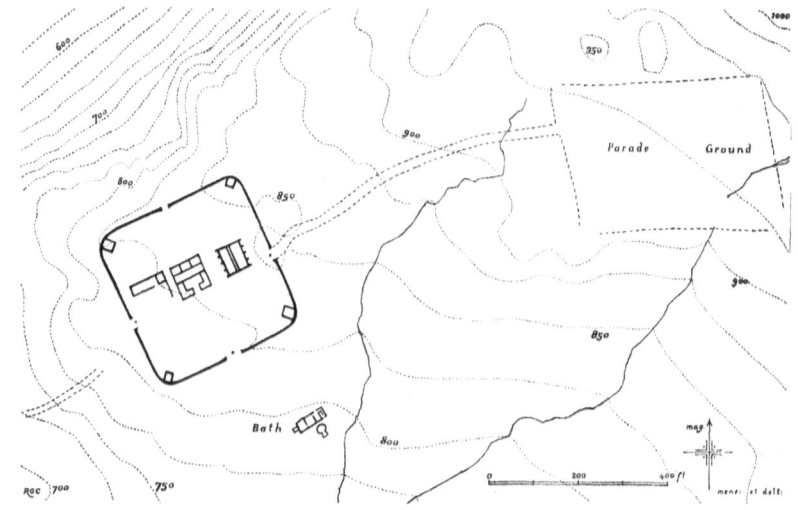

Fig. 2. Plan of Hardknot Castle.

apparent omission of Hardknot in Iter X suggests the possibility that in the late second or early third century when the Itineraries were drawn up the site may have been uninhabited ; and that again suggested to me the desirability of seeing what could be done to determine the date of the occupation from the finds. These were the property of the late Lord Muncaster, who owned the site and found labour for the excavations ; and it was well known that they were preserved at Muncaster Castle.

Owing to the war, an opportunity to inspect them did not arrive till 1920. Ten years before, they had received some attention from Haverfield, who reported that they were disappointing—no Samian to speak of, very few coins, no inscriptions, but some coarse pottery types pointing to a first-century occupation, a suggestion confirmed by coins of Antony and Domitian.[1] But in 1910 very little was known about the accurate dating of Romano-British coarse pottery. Mr. James Curle's work at Newstead, which marked the beginning of the scientific study of such pottery, had already pointed the way, but it was not till about 1913 or 1914 that sufficient evidence had been accumulated and published to make the dating of a site from coarse pottery alone a possibility worthy of serious consideration. This possibility was especially due to the work of 1911 and succeeding years at Corbridge, at Wroxeter, and at certain well-stratified sites near Birdoswald on Hadrian's Wall. I therefore hoped that by bringing this further knowledge to bear on the Hardknot finds, always supposing these finds had really been preserved in their entirety, it would be possible to date the occupation of the fort within reasonable limits.

On my visit to Muncaster Castle I found to my great satisfaction the whole mass of finds, down to the humblest potsherd, for the most part neatly packed in paper parcels and labelled in the hands of C. W. Dymond and the Rev. W. S. Calverley, both Fellows of this Society, who directed the work, and both now some years dead. Considering the date at which the excavations were done and the differences of opinion which unfortunately divided the directors, it was an impressive thing to see with what care they had united to preserve and label these bushels of fragments, to themselves quite unintelligible, in the hope that some future inquirer might be able to make use of them. The parcels had never been opened, previous inquirers (if, indeed, there were any besides Haverfield) having only inspected those sherds which had not been packed up; so that I was the first person to go through the bulk of the pottery.

On examining the whole of the material, I was at once struck by the fact that the fort had not been occupied after the second century. The earliest types of pottery were those which are everywhere in Scotland and the north of England associated with the campaigns of Agricola; the latest date somewhere not very late in the second century. On a closer inspection I felt obliged to date the occupation as lasting from A.D. 80 to 120; that is, to ascribe the origin of the fort to Agricola and to regard it as having been continuously occupied after his recall till about the time of Hadrian's visit to Britain. The evidence for this dating is set forth below.

The upper date I provisionally identify with the campaign of Agricola in 79. The evidence for this, apart from the inscription which may perhaps have

---

[1] MS. notes preserved in the Haverfield library at Oxford; *Eph. Epigr.* ix, p. 568. An inscription was once visible on the site, reading GRIC .. LA .. COII (*C.I.L.* vii, 334; *Proceedings*, 1st. Ser., iii, 225), but there is nothing to indicate whether Julius Agricola, Calpurnius Agricola, or somebody else is named.

borne his name, consists of a few potsherds of strikingly early appearance, described and figured below (fig. 3, nos. 1–4). If, as may well be the case, these sherds are only isolated specimens of their period lingering on into a time when later types had almost ousted them, the pottery would tend to suggest that Hardknot was really built ten or even twenty years later. This possibility must be borne in mind ; but if such a theory is accepted it will entail important consequences in the shape of a very large scheme of fortification carried out in the north of England about the year 100, midway between the Agricolan and Hadrianic schemes, a movement for which we have no scrap of literary evidence, to which a mass of relics must be ascribed which have generally been considered Agricolan. For quite small movements of this kind about the year 100 or later there is some archaeological evidence, but as yet not much ; what there is appears to me still insufficient to outweigh the general probability that a fort situated like Hardknot, and certainly flourishing by about 100, was built by Agricola, who must have paid some attention to this piece of country in 79 and did, as we know from Tacitus, secure his conquests by means of a network of such forts. On the other hand, the potsherds at Hardknot that seem to date before 100 are much outnumbered by those that can probably be ascribed to the years 100–20 ; and the Agricolan date of Hardknot cannot be very confidently asserted on the strength of the pottery evidence alone.

The lower date of about A.D. 120 depends on a number of arguments of which that from coarse pottery is conclusive by itself, though the others serve to corroborate it. We shall consider the others first.

1. In ground plan the fort is a small square enclosure, not unlike a considerable number of first-century forts in shape and arrangement. It had a stone rampart with an earth bank behind it (a feature common to first- and early second-century forts) and its general appearance on the plan suggests a Flavian-Trajanic date. Now we have reason to believe that when these square early forts were reoccupied, as many were reoccupied, in the time of Hadrian they were generally razed to the ground and rebuilt on a wholly new plan. We do not, it is true, know very much about this subject yet. But the familiar plans at Bar Hill and Newstead, where in each case an Agricolan fort was thrown down and a new one on a more or less different pattern built by the Antonine engineers, find an excellent parallel not a dozen miles from Hardknot at Ambleside, where the explorations of the Cumberland and Westmorland Society [1] from 1913 to 1915 revealed a small squarish fort of the late first century, placed, just as Hardknot is placed, on a suitable plot of ground to which its plan is subtly adapted, and on the top of that a second-century fort, a good deal larger, oblong in shape like the forts of Hadrian's Wall and built upon a platform of artificially levelled

[1] Excavation reports in *Cumb. and West. Trans.* N.S. xiv, xv, xvi, xxi.

ground. Now if the site of Hardknot had been reoccupied as part of Hadrian's scheme, it is difficult to imagine that the buildings would not have been razed, the site levelled up, and a fort of the well-known second-century pattern built over it. This was not done; there is only one fort at Hardknot, and that is the first-century fort.

2. There is, secondly, the argument from coins. On this I lay little stress, for some coins may have been overlooked; but it is at least remarkable that the only coins found, setting aside two illegible ones, were a silver Antony, a denarius of Domitian dated to A.D. 95, and a brass of Trajan.

3. Of even less value is the argument from Samian pottery, of which extremely little was found. There is one tolerably complete vessel, a dish (Dragendorff 18) bearing the mark RVFFI·M. This potter appears to be undoubtedly a South Gaulish Flavian manufacturer,[1] but that does not prove that the deposit in which the vessel occurs is limited to the Flavian period or even belongs to that period at all; Mr. Curle reports wares of this very potter in Antonine deposits at Newstead. There is also one piece of figured Samian bearing an early Lezoux pattern (Déchelette 736) found at Wroxeter in a deposit of 80–130.

4. The only evidence whose bulk and character put it beyond dispute is that of the coarse pottery. Here not only are definitely late wares, like the so-called 'pitted' ware of the fourth century, the mortaria with 'hammer-head' rim, and the hard pipeclay fabrics with or without painted patterns, entirely absent, but it is to be observed that of second-century wares the characteristically Antonine types are almost wholly wanting, and only those are present which, when found in Hadrianic or Antonine deposits, are recognizable as survivals from the reign of Trajan.

To say this involves a claim to a somewhat close dating of certain pottery-types, and consequently it is desirable to review the types in detail in the hope of obtaining further light in the shape of criticisms by other students of coarse pottery.

We may begin with mortaria (fig. 3). The general type of mortarium is a heavy, hemispherical bowl a foot or less in diameter, having its inner surface thickly set with particles of hard stone to aid the trituration of meal or the like, and furnished with a massive rim. In the dating of mortaria the shape of the rim is the most useful guide, though the quality and colour of the clay, the character of the grit, and other indications are also of value.

Hardknot yields several mortaria (1–4) of very hard, rather gritty, fabric

---

[1] Déchelette, *Vases céramiques ornés de la Gaule romaine*, vol. i, p. 84, ascribes him to La Graufe-senque. Messrs. Oswald and Pryce, *Terra Sigillata*, pp. 82, 122, 172, s.v. Rufus, give instances of the name on Drag. 29 and 37 (La Graufesenque and Montans, Nero to Domitian) and on Drag. 24/25.

with wide, thin, and almost flat rims. This is a first-century type. It begins losing its purity even towards the end of the century, and by the end of the century the rim is rapidly getting thicker and less flat. It is very seldom that one of these flat rims is found lingering on into a Hadrianic site; one resembling them occurred in the early stratum at High House Turret. These Hardknot specimens look to me definitely earlier than anything that has been found at the certainly Agricolan sites of Corbridge and Newstead, and they therefore constitute the pottery evidence, such as it is, for the Agricolan date of Hardknot.

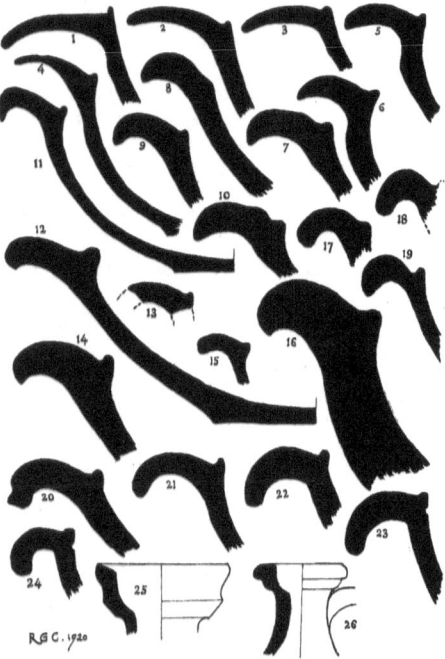

Fig. 3.   Mortaria and two Jugs from Hardknot ($\frac{1}{2}$).

The great majority of the Hardknot mortaria, however, belong to a type which has developed out of this flat rim, a type whose *floruit* appears to be about the years 90–120. Many of these Hardknot mortaria can be paralleled from the Wroxeter deposits of that period, and they have decided affinities with certain types found in the earliest strata on Hadrian's Wall and even on Scottish Antonine sites. Thus two mortaria, extremely like one of the latest Hardknot varieties (fig. 3, no. 17), are figured by Mr. Curle as coming from the Antonine fort at Newstead (nos. 11 and 12, see fig. 4). Similarly there are parallels between Hardknot no. 6 (fig. 3) and a High House Milecastle Hadrianic type (103 in fig. 4); another High House Milecastle type (101, fig. 4) resembles fig. 3, no. 22 from Hardknot, and yet another (100, fig. 4) resembles fig. 3, no. 20. But in all these cases the rule seems to hold good that either the Hardknot type is earlier in character than its analogue, or else the analogue is exceptionally early as compared with the associated finds while the Hardknot specimen looks exceptionally late. We have therefore, it would appear, an example of overlapping types, which were at Hardknot associated with earlier patterns and in the middle of the century with later, while their period of commonest occurrence was probably about 120.

In searching Hadrian's Wall for close parallels with the later Hardknot wares—in searching, that is, for deposits in which late Hardknot types are the rule rather than the exception occurring among later patterns—we find such parallels only in the pre-Hadrianic forts on the Stanegate, viz. Throp and Haltwhistle Burn. Here, in forts built after the year 110 and abandoned about 120, mortaria closely resembling those from Hardknot are not the exception, as they are in Hadrianic deposits, but the rule. Indeed, every single mortarium found at these two forts might have come from Hardknot, and if they were shuffled among the Hardknot types it would be impossible for any one to pick them out on the ground of typological differences. Thus Haltwhistle Burn no. 3 (fig. 4) is practically Hardknot 6 (fig. 3); Throp 1, 2, and 3 (fig. 4) are hardly distinguishable from nos. 20-3 in fig. 3, which form the most characteristic late group among the Hardknot mortaria. There is nothing at Hardknot later than these; which seems to imply that the evacuation of Hardknot Castle dates about the same time as that of Throp and Haltwhistle Burn—at, or soon before, the building of Hadrian's Wall.

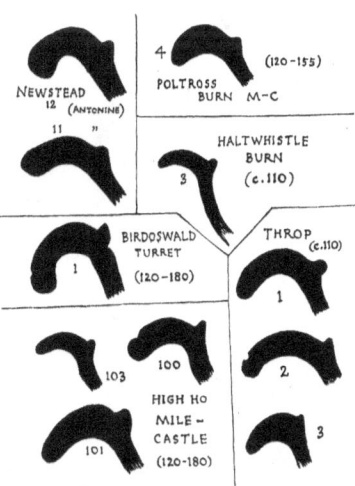

Fig. 4. Other Mortaria (⅓).

Turning to the bowls, we find that the Hardknot specimens are almost all of the carinated pattern with a flat or nearly flat rim, and the body cylindrical above and conical below, with a definite angle at the junction. Now this is a familiar type of the first century which lasts into the second but disappears completely and abruptly in the earlier part of the latter century. Thus in the Antonine fort at Newstead it is wholly absent, and in the Hadrianic strata on the Wall it only occurs exceptionally, for there are several examples in the Poltross Burn Milecastle, and nowhere else; whereas at pre-Hadrianic sites on the Wall (Corbridge early deposits, Haltwhistle Burn) it is of normal occurrence.

Poltross Burn is the only proved case of its appearance after 120. That is to say, it had disappeared in all but exceptional cases by 120, and altogether by 140, its place being taken by the 'pie-dish' bowl with straight sloping sides and a small flat rim, a type of vessel which generally carries a lattice ornament on the outside. That is the type in use at Newstead in the Antonine fort, and elsewhere. Now these 'pie-dish' bowls, very common in all mid-second-century sites, are entirely absent from Hardknot. The nearest is fig. 5, no. 44, which, however, is not the real type but one transitional to it, with a thick lip and no lattice ornament. The Hardknot series thus ends while the carinated bowl is still in its prime and before the 'pie-dish' has begun to take its place. This implies that it ends not later than where the earliest deposits on Hadrian's Wall begin. The Hardknot series seems to pass over into the Poltross Burn series without overlap and without appreciable break. For the Hardknot series includes hundreds of bowls closely akin to those found at Poltross Burn; in type they are less clean and sharp, in fabric less hard, than the early bowls from Corbridge and Newstead, and this brings their date nearer to the Hadrianic period than to the Agricolan or even the post-Agricolan Corbridge deposits.

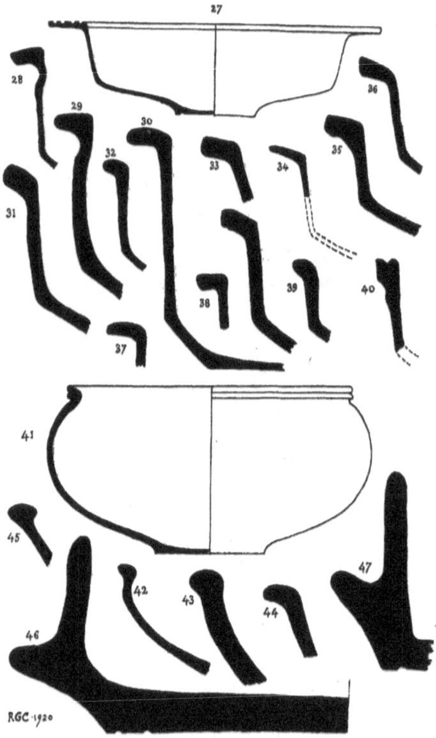

Fig. 5. Bowls from Hardknot (½).

On the other hand, certain of the Hardknot bowls seem earlier than the immediately pre-Hadrianic period; such are the very fine bowl 27, and the two heavy but hard and well-made *casserole*-shaped dishes (46, 47). I know of no parallel to these two, but their style is that of the late first century. The independent evidence of the bowls thus permits an occupation dating back as far as Agricola, though not necessarily so far, and points very clearly to an evacuation about the time of the construction of Hadrian's Wall or a little earlier.

The various types of cooking-pot and beaker need not detain us long. By far the commonest are 48 and 49 (fig. 7), which are characteristic of the late first century and the beginning of the second. All the types 48–73 fall into this category; many of them linger into the Hadrianic, some even into the Antonine period, but in that case they are exceptions among prevalent later patterns, whereas at Hardknot they are the rule and occur in large numbers. A special problem, however, is presented by nos. 74-8, of which there are altogether, perhaps, half a dozen specimens. This is a typically Antonine pattern. It lasts with hardly any visible modification throughout the later second century and the third, and in deposits of the Hadrian-Antonine period it has already more or less completely expelled the 'neckless' types here represented by 48-73. Thus at Newstead it is the only kind of cooking-pot in use. This means that by 140 it is fully established; but it remains to be seen whether it came into use before 120 or whether its presence at Hardknot indicates a continued occupation after about that date. Fortunately this question can be answered with confidence. Two necked cooking-pots of just this pattern were found in the pre-Hadrianic fort at Haltwhistle Burn and three in the corresponding fort at Throp. In the latter site, it is true, a few intrusive potsherds of later date were found; but these three were not considered to be intrusive. Here again,

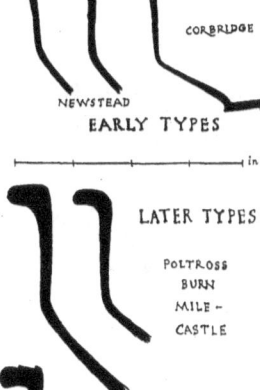

Fig. 6. Other bowls (⅓).

therefore, the pre-Hadrianic Stanegate forts supply an accurate parallel with the latest phase of the occupation at Hardknot.

This evidence has been stated in detail because this is the first occasion on which a Romano-British site has been dated on the strength of coarse pottery alone; and in view of the present condition of the study of such pottery, and of the scepticism—a reasonable and necessary scepticism—with which the students of such pottery have generally found themselves confronted when they have ventured to predict the possibility of such datings, I feel it desirable to expose the whole process to the fullest possible criticism. The conclusion so far obtained is that the occupation of Hardknot Castle extended from Agricola, or from a date soon after Agricola, down to a date shortly before Hadrian began to reorganize the frontier system.   The pottery alone seems to me to prove an occupation from about 90 to about 120, or—since no one can claim to date by coarse pottery to within a year or two—from a date in the last twenty years of the first century to a date between 110 and 120, and perhaps nearer 120 than 110.   On general grounds, as I have explained above, I find it easier to put the date of foundation back to Agricola (which the pottery, I think, permits) than to assume that the fort was built about 95, with all that such an assumption implies; but that is a matter on which future research alone can give us certainty.   For the present we must add Hardknot to the list of 'post-Agricolan'

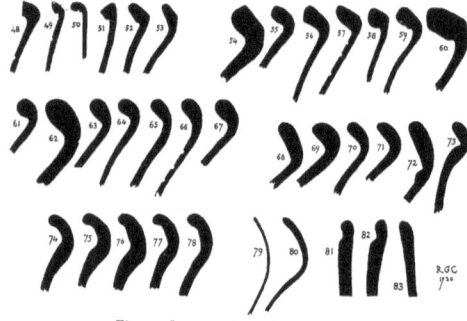

Fig. 7. Jars, &c., from Hardknot (⅓).

sites, in the sense of sites which continued to be occupied in the interval between Agricola and Hadrian.

This is a valuable conclusion, because the history of this interval is now receiving a good deal of attention.   Quite lately it was the accepted view that Agricola's campaigns were fruitless in the sense that their conquests were abandoned on his recall, and that it was reserved for Hadrian to push forward once more and to reoccupy sites which had lain vacant for thirty or forty years.   When Mr. Curle found indications which led him to think that Newstead must have been held for an appreciable time after Agricola's withdrawal, his conclusions were by no means universally accepted; they were, indeed, challenged by no less an authority than Dragendorff (in the *Journal of Roman Studies*, vol. i, p. 135).   But since then discoveries have proceeded rapidly.   At Inchtuthill, Camelon, and Ardoch, Dr. Macdonald has shown [1] that there were long post-Agricolan occupations, long enough to involve important reconstructions.   At Inchtuthill there are traces of three distinct forts, all falling in the Flavian-Trajanic period.   The number is interesting because it recalls that at Hardknot three superimposed floor-levels were found in the corner towers and perhaps elsewhere.   The fact is certain, in spite of the denial of one of the excavators.   The three floors found, about the same time, at Mucklebank Turret on

---

[1] Since this paper was written Dr. Macdonald has embodied his conclusions in a paper read at Oxford, and now published in *J. R. S.*, vol. ix.

Hadrian's Wall by the late J. P. Gibson, and later at Aesica, Poltross Burn, and elsewhere, suggested that the Hardknot floors were to be equated with these Hadrianic and post-Hadrianic strata; but now that they are clearly proved to be wholly pre-Hadrianic it is tempting to connect them with the three forts at Inchtuthill, on which hypothesis the lowest Hardknot floor would be Agricolan. The excavators at Hardknot unfortunately did not keep the pottery from the various floors separate.

In the north of England the same post-Agricolan occupation reappears. At Corbridge the Agricolan fort went on well into the reign of Trajan. At other sites along the Stanegate, forts were actually built during this period after the turn of the century. Farther south again, there are post-Agricolan occupations at Slack and Castleshaw; but the interval between these southern forts and the Stanegate has yielded no evidence on this subject except the fact that Hardknot also had a post-Agricolan history. This fact, however, is significant and points to others. The northern end of the Tenth Iter now appears to be Agricolan. At Ambleside we found an apparently Agricolan earthwork; at Watercrook there are some indications of first-century pottery; the evidence at Hardknot we have just reviewed; and at Ravenglass I have picked up a water-worn scrap of a Flavian mortarium. The whole line of road and forts is thus apparently a first-century scheme. And of this scheme one member, Hardknot, is now seen to have been kept going till close on Hadrian's arrival; presumably, that is, till the great disaster which befell the Roman garrisons at the beginning of Hadrian's reign and was the reason of his visit to Britain.

Now if Hardknot was retained during the post-Agricolan interval, it follows that other places in the district were retained also. Inchtuthill, Ardoch, Camelon, Newstead, and Corbridge are all important places, which would have to be held if the country was to be garrisoned at all. They are all strategic centres. But Hardknot is merely a link in a chain of forts along a road. It has no strategic significance whatever. It is not a centre for anything. It cannot possibly have been held, and no one would want to hold it even if he could, unless the other forts along the line, or at least a good many of them, were held too. If Ravenglass was held, and if Watercrook was held, then we can understand a garrison at Hardknot, but not otherwise. Ambleside we know was not held. The first-century remains are definite but scanty; there is every mark of a short occupation, and the whole early fort is sealed by a thick bed of silt laid down by the Rothay between its abandonment and its second-century re-occupation. The conclusion forces itself upon us that in the period between Agricola and Hadrian garrisons were maintained at Ravenglass and at the important road-junction of Watercrook; and that it was felt necessary to hold an intermediate fort as well. Ambleside was too low-lying and wet; so Hardknot, though in other ways less convenient, was held instead. After 120 when Hadrian reorganized the district, Ambleside was taken in hand, and the whole fort raised above flood-level on a platform of dredged gravel; this made Ambleside a habitable site, and Hardknot was allowed to lie waste.

But it is impossible to look at the map and maintain that an Agricolan and post-Agricolan occupation which involved these four forts on the Tenth Iter did not go farther. If Agricola planned the Tenth Iter and built its forts, we can hardly suppose that he planned it as his main line of march and of communications. If he was advancing northwards by way of Lancashire, it can hardly be doubted that he used the Lune gorge, and that the northern end of the Tenth Iter had a merely subsidiary importance, being designed at once to penetrate and secure the mountain district on his flank and to tap an exceptionally useful port. But this means that the series Lancaster (or Overborough or more likely both), Low Borrow Bridge, Brougham, and Old Penrith is partly or wholly an Agricolan series, and not only Agricolan but post-Agricolan.

From this point of view it may reasonably be argued that the post-Agricolan occupation of Hardknot, a secondary fort on a secondary line, proves *a fortiori* the post-Agricolan occupation of half a dozen other sites at the very least in the same district. And thus Hardknot, because of its very unimportance as a military centre, gains an additional importance as a link in a chain of evidence, and suggests not only that the Cumberland and Westmorland district was held after Agricola's departure, but that it was held on a very large scale and with an intensity of which our previous evidence in other districts gave us no idea.

It remains to verify this suggestion. Off the lines of the Wall and the Tenth Iter, excavations have been very rare in this district; but my own short dig at Papcastle in 1912 produced some mortaria which seem to me certainly pre-Hadrianic, and showed that there was an earlier fort underlying the one we were exploring. This earlier fort may well have been Agricolan. Nothing else has been done; for the attempt to dig Low Borrow Bridge in the eighties and Haverfield's excavations at the temporary camp of Caermote in 1900 have left no pottery, not even descriptions of what they found. Chance finds, like those at Maryport and recently at Mawbray, are unlikely to tap the lower strata of a site. I think we may claim to have shown that a campaign of digging would reveal a very important and widespread post-Agricolan occupation in the north-west of England; that recent work on the Tenth Iter has completed the first stage in this campaign, and that the next stage can be carried out whenever the means are forthcoming.